THE BACK DOCK

and other poems

Joanne Saltzman

ISBN: 1502404796
ISBN 13: 9781502404794
Library of Congress Control Number: 2014916732
CreateSpace Independent Pub. Platform
North Charleston, South Carolina

For my grandfather
Herman H. Butterman

Acknowledgements

Deep gratitude and abundant thanks to my daughter, Judy Hammett, for invaluable help in putting this collection together; to April Bogdon for sustained support; to Edith Sobel for encouragement that mattered; and to my husband, Alan Saltzman, for giving meaningful input when I most needed it.

Contents

Romance

1990's

FAMILY

REFLECTION

1960's

1970's

1980's

1990's

2000's

Romance

There Is the Time

There is the time to be alone
And know the excitement
Of solitude.
There is the time to laugh and sing
And know the elation of happiness.
There is the time to cry hard
And know the bitter taste
Of despair.
There is the time to think profoundly
And know the worth of knowledge
And books.
There is the time to love and give
And know the feeling
Of being complete.
There is the time to live
And it is now.

A Thought

When the sun penetrates
My skin without mercy
It hurts and I cover myself.
When the sun caresses me
With a tender glow
I willingly yield.
And I am like that
With you, my darling,
Except that when you burn me,
I cannot find the shade.

THE TWO OF US

Grass pressed beneath us.
You can't change anything.
Coming down the hill,
It rolls out of nothing.
When did it start?
We smell moist blades.
Can you forgive me?
Twigs under us,
Snapping at me.
Did you forget?
Warm air fanning me,
Bumping up against you.
The two of us not fitting
In the circle of sunlight.
Your legs, my shoulders
In the shaded part,
Until the light shifts,
Or we do.

Do You Remember?

I can't remember now
Which night it was or
What words we were using
At each other.
I don't remember losing
My spirit to fight with you,
But I did, even though
I don't usually lose things.
I remember loving you.
I still do, but how?

Everything Leaves Her

Everything leaves her cold.
And what about you?
You could have warmed her once.
Now her hair hangs like dead bark
Around her face,
While you nourish yourself,
By yourself,
Like a spider at spinning.

Oh Morning, Come

Will morning ever come?
Not for me right away.
I hunger to see it,
Eyes closed and focused,
My body intent on it.
Oh morning, come.
Bring wet leaves and breakfast.
Cradle me with sunrise.
Make the surrounding
Darkness disappear.
Oh morning, come.

Empty Benches

If we could talk
To each other
Would you tell me
What I want to hear?
Empty benches
In the park
Moist at dawn
Dusty by night
Waiting for pigeons
And old men
With a little more time.
We could sit
Just long enough to talk.

About Today

A train goes by
But we wait.
Streams flow with us,
Currents through me.
The trapeze has come
Back to the ground.
Today I almost told you
After the cotton candy
And the blind magician,
But you were crying
So instead, I put
The rabbit in your lap.

LET'S

Come play with me,
I am still a child inside.
Aren't you flying kites
Under that suit?
Warm wind against our faces,
Blowing away the time.
Let's laugh a lot
Because we can,
And let's not stop.

MY BATH WATER

Tears for you drip gently
Into my bath water.
Silent sobs make ripples
You don't see.
The candles were lit
With quixotic prayer.
Fresh yearning buoys
My injured heart
Until my bath water
Slips, like sand, away.

Meeting You

You are buried within me,
A stranger I have always known
And may not see again.
From one river, our blood flows.
You might not choose me,
But in essence, I am with you.
Quell the fear that bridles you,
And see me again.

Between Us

I'm drawn to you
Without reason
Just soul to soul
Like a wave
To the shoreline,
And then another.
Something exists
Between us,
Casting a reel
Over the time
We've yet to have
Between us.

WINTER IN THE WINDOW

Winter in the window
Doesn't chill us.
My tenderness becomes
Passion in your arms
Like a crescendo
That must repeat.
Time cannot penetrate
The nucleus of this moment
When our silhouette
Undulates upon the wall.

Your Fingers

Your fingers have humiliated me.
A siren song of hollow charm
Came out of you, like music
From a player piano.
You transgressed my
Precious territory,
Like a dog sniffing a spot
He decides against.
You wiped your neck
With my loyalty.

Your Words

I trusted you with my heart
And you trashed it.
I didn't deserve
The callousness you chose.
You said you wouldn't
Waste my time. In fact,
You had a plethora
Of lines designed
To reel me under you.
Your words were as shallow
As those you condemn.
I want to believe in you again,
But it will take blood
You may not have to let.

WHEN THE HEART IS BROKEN

When the heart is broken
Nothing bleeds,
But something deeper smarts.
Continuous monologues play,
Unrehearsed, on the mind's
Silent stage.
Tears that seem perpetual
Cannot reach the wound.

I'm Nobody's Valentine

I'm nobody's valentine
And that makes me sad
I'm hurting for tenderness and
Love real bad
And not in some statement
Of words abstract
I want to be somebody's
Valentine in fact
I want so to matter
To my valentine
In the most special way
For the longest time
To mean what we say
And feel what we mean
I don't want to die
Without having been seen

FOR ALAN

I wished on so many stars
In skies East and West
I begged starlight star bright
Please, please make my wish
Come true tonight.
On nights stars were everywhere,
On nights when I had to search for one,
I yearned with aching soul
For a true love like in the fairy tales.
A Prince Charming who would set
Eyes on me
And love me devotedly
And whom I would love entirely as well,
A fit that seemed too romantically idealistic,
Too much the stuff of myth.
Yet, when I was long past the age
Of wishing on stars,
You came walking along the beach to me,
Then I towards you,
Then we together,
Sensing, knowing that the stars, after all,
Had heard.

FAMILY

The Reunion

The man had never seen his son,
Though ten
Swift years had flown
Since first the child unto the world his strong,
Young face had shown.
The father looked upon his son his heart
Increased its pace
As he beheld the loving eyes, the warm
And friendly face.
A gentle hand reached out to touch its father's
Hand at last
Away they walked and neither cared if ten long
Years had passed.

WAITING

The sky was blue
The sun was bright
The flowers danced
Their petals white.
The man walked up
And down the way
He worried now
And prayed all day
And hoped his
Wife was safe and well
And that the doctor
Soon would tell
Him that his loving
Wife and he
Were parents of
Their child to be!

Letting Waves Roll In

Two tiny hands I'm holding,
We are letting waves roll in.
Jessie squeals each time the water
Goes back out
And she dances in the muddy sand
That's left.
Judy dances too, till the water
Starts to come.
The icy foam is near now,
She is breathless.
She squats to let the water
Touch more of her.

While Rocking Judy

You are soft in my arms
I tenderly hold you
You want to be rocked.
On the curtain
I watch our silhouettes
Still in disbelief that
You are no longer inside me,
And I rock, singing,
"Mommy's rocking Judy,
Mommy's rocking Judy."

For Cody

After you passed, I still believed
I would see you again.
Sometimes, I'm sure
They meant someone else.
I long to talk with you.
I think you knew how much
I loved you.
But maybe you didn't.
Maybe I treated you like the others did.
I never thought of you that way,
As "help".

Daughter, Listen

Daughter, listen to me
My words have to stick,
For as long as you live
So will I.
I hear my grandmothers.
Between my ears
They live on.
When my eyes are closed,
Their voices sound
Exactly as they were.
And I listen,
Much like a bird does,
Tilting my head slightly
So as to catch the tones,
And every cherished word.

Tea, Dry

One rider missing from the carousel,
And the sky has no balloons.
On the streets we used to shiver down,
I still expect to feel
Her venerable arm in mine.
The cadence of our years
Reverberates within me.
Her face rests in my mind,
Like mountain snow the sun never melts.
My grandmother ordered her tea dry,
And sometimes, I had to remind her
To dip the bag,
Because there was so much
She wanted to tell me.

Happy Birthday, Grandma

Happy Birthday, Grandma.
You would have been eighty-three.
You should have been.
I wonder if you can see me.
I guess it is possible.
I have continued on,
Fifteen years so far.
My grief became
Another root grounding me.
Sometimes I miss you
More than I can bear.
Today I do.
You would have loved
My daughter,
And she you.
You've never left me.

The Dolls in Longchamps

Every Sunday, the family
Ate at Longchamps.
She ordered lamb chops
And couldn't sit still
Until they came.
When the grown-up conversation
Began to drown her,
She was allowed
To go look at the dolls.
They breathed the air
She wanted.
She knew they could see her.
They said,
"You're going to be one of us
When you're big."
She was sure of that.
Once, her grandmother said
She could have one of the dolls
But she couldn't pick.
The dolls in Longchamps
Lived perfectly on the shelf,
And one little girl
With freckles and messy curls
Believed they were happy.

My Daughter's Sorrow

I long for your sorrow,
That it be mine alone.
My eyes want to wince
With your sadness.
My heart begs for
The burden you feel.
Yet I am helpless,
Like a rock that
Cannot be a tree.

GRANDPA'S LOVE

I need you here.
I almost see you in the doorway
And that comforts me.
It's as if your boundless love
Has replaced the air in my room.
I need to talk to you.
I have thirteen years
Of silent sentences.
What rubs is
When you could have heard them,
They hadn't even occurred to me.
I was still wiping your
Wet kisses from my face
And shoving the itchy blanket
Of your love to one side.

FOR JUDY AT SIXTEEN

In the sound of the sea
I hear my soul
And in your face
I see it.
Time has brought you
To the threshold I once crossed.
You step, uncertainly,
Away from childhood,
Cheeks flushed, eyes ready.
You tread without a path
While I, fervently,
Pull stones and twigs
From your midst.

SUNDAY

I miss you most on Sunday.
Waking has no melody.
The air is quiet
Without your eager voice
On the phone.
The day proceeds,
Empty minutes with not even
One second of you,
Except inside me
Where every heartbeat
Is for both of us, Mom.

The Visit

Last night, no, this morning
I saw you in a dream.
I knew you waited inside.
I entered the house,
Desperate to see you.
Others tried to calm me,
To make the visit social.
I searched each room
Calling, "Mom."
Then I saw you
Dancing towards me.
I gripped you
For one everlasting moment.

THE CASHEW SISTERS

Joan Ruth Ruth Joan
Ruth Joan Joan Ruth
Taking life's turns with each other
Laughing, talking, crying
Talking, whispering, smiling
Book-ends guarding volumes
Of loving memories.

J

Copper hair everywhere
Milk chocolate eyes
That question and know.
Hand, like a warmed glass,
Holding it, the grounding in the universe.

NOVEMBER

Again it is November.
Inescapable eleventh darkest month
That sinks beneath the calendar.
Again, it is November.

ANNIE'S PEARLS

Annie's pearls are still warm
From long ago when she wore them.
They carry her love,
Each one of the fifty-seven jewels
On a single strand.
They are tiny mirrors in the light
Rich with the part of Annie
That stayed in the pearls
So that her beloved Kelly
Could hold them in one hand
And feel her grandma still with her.
Annie's pearls are on my neck now.
They carry her essence
And Kelly's love for me,
Each one of the fifty-seven jewels
On a single strand.

Again

It will never be right that you're gone,
That I'm not hearing your laugh;
Or hugging you as only an only daughter
Holds her mother.
It will never be right that you don't know
Your granddaughter has a daughter
Whose middle name is Love.
The "L" is for you.
She sits at your piano
Albeit in a diaper
And bangs on the keys you played,
Starting the music again.

WATCHING EVE SLEEP

How did I make it
To this unimaginable bliss?
Countless, seemingly endless lifetimes,
States of being, schools, marriages, divorces,
Child rearing, teen rearing, jobs, days spent,
Nights slept or not, dreams, conversations,
Incalculable thoughts come and gone,
World travels, homes bought and sold.
I have done so much,
But I have never been so much.
I am filled with infinite gratitude
To be here now, watching Eve sleep.

WAX PAPER

Whenever I use wax paper,
I think immediately of you
Your gentle hands
Wrapping goodies prepared
Solely for me
In the wax paper
You always used.
Your hands soft and with
Purple bulging veins I'd trace
With plump nail bitten fingers
Searching for wisdom,
Sure of it.

Sharing Oat Squares

It is nearly forty years
Since I lay, exhausted,
In the delivery room
Watching the miracle
Of your birth
In a high placed mirror.
As your head emerged,
And I saw my baby's
Dear face for the first time,
I still didn't know
If you were the girl
My heart believed I carried.
Then, in just seconds,
You were out of me
And the nurse said,
"It's a girl"
And right then,
You started to cry
Just a little, not a wail,
And I said, "It's okay, Judy."

Now we sit in a hotel bathroom,
Quietly sharing oat squares
So as not to wake the others
Still asleep this early Sunday morning.
You sit on the tub's side,
I on the lid closed toilet.
Your face is calm and loving
And as dear to me today.
We whisper, engaged,
Our thoughts flowing
Our bond like our breath.

Happy Birthday, Mom

Happy birthday, Mom.
You would have been eighty-seven today.
I think you're glad you're not!
Aging was not one of your goals.
Living passionately originally was.
And so you did for sixty-nine years.
Each moment fueled by the unique
Energy that was you.
I miss you today.
I miss you every day.
I have immeasurable gratitude for
Coming from you,
For being of you
Your egg to my conception
First your matter
Then mine.

STANDING ON THE ROCK

No time for sentimentality
That is for others who are not
Standing on the rock
That never cracks
Even in the rain.
Others have time to laugh
To look at nothing for a while
But that man on that rock
Begins each day of his life
Claiming a creed.
He says, "The divine spirit in me
Salutes the divine spirit in you."

The Gift from My Mother

Thank you for
The gift
From the stalk plant
You gave me
Twenty-four years ago
When it was four feet tall
And now touches the ceiling
The green tongue leaves had
Given only one flower
In the mid 1990's
Until now, November 2012
Just days before your
Twentieth yahrzeit
The plant gives
Three wondrous
Flowers with
Dizzyingly gorgeous fragrances
A bouquet from you
To let us know
You are flying everywhere
Eternally blossoming soul

OUR LAST CONVERSATION

We have had our last conversation.
Me at home in New Jersey,
You in your den in Santa Rosa;
I asked if you were okay,
You said yes, fine.
You sounded done,
For the first time in your
Almost ninety-two years
Of living,
I heard you sound
Like you were done.
Plain, simple
No regrets
No tragedy
No turning back.

Nobody's Child

Nobody's child
Nobody's daughter
Quiet
No pillars surrounding
Nothing displacing the air
The air is everywhere
They are nowhere now

REFLECTION

To Be Alive

To have some goal you want to reach,
To act, to dance, to nurse, or teach;
To realize that you are unique,
To learn a trade, to have technique
In something which you like to do,
To seek the path that's best for you,
To read, to see if life is grand,
For only then will you understand,
To have some aim you are working for
Is to be alive and so much more.

THE FUTURE

How often I wonder what path I'll take
When there are decisions and plans to make.
Perhaps as I reach a womanly age
I'll take all my talents and
Display them on stage
With characters who are from every new play
And scenes I'll perform with the start of each day.
The public will rave and the papers will shout
That this is the finest new starlet that's out
And as I will sit on a plane I will be
Hollywood bound, movie pictures for me
To love in and live in and die in too,
This is all but a dream of what I'd like to do!

TIME, IMMORTAL SOUL

Time, Immortal Soul!
Forever you must wander
Your journey never done.
Have you ever slept;
Or stopped to shade the sun
That glistens in your eyes,
As onward you must go?
Time, Immortal Soul,
'Tis you I pity so!

AND EVERYDAY

And everyday I wake to see
The morning clear and bright.
And everyday towards six o'clock,
Earth receives her night.
And everyday my building stands
Its color always grey.
In fact it's just my soul that changes
Each and every day.

THE POOR

The rich see them as ragged,
A tired and hungry race
With grimy hands that linger,
To itch a drawn out face.
The rich laugh at these paupers
Who waver on life's thread,
Struggling for survival,
Begging for their bread.
But their poverty is material
And this they can well bear.
For poor as well as rich can feel
The yearn to love and share.
And so each man stands equal
In the eyes of the Lord above,
For what is wealth and social stance
Without the warmth of love?

DEATH

He came to me in friendly dress and yet
His hands were cold.
He smiled at me, his gums were black
As I had once been told.
He stretched his bony hand towards mine,
I withdrew a little ways.
And then rose I to share with him
My eternal lonely days.

A Memory

If ever there was a sight that
During childhood I remember,
It's of a horse that once I mounted
Came my sixth September.
The country air was chilled and
Leaves swayed gently towards my feet.
And sun's warm heat did blanket
Every flower smelling sweet.
The day was perfect for most
Any pastime one might choose,
And I, with hair so long and limp,
With gaily buckled shoes,
Decided that a walk along the
Golden shore would be
The finest entertainment that
My eyes could ever see.
And that is how it came to pass
That on that lovely morn,
I managed to sneak by the maid,
My strange account now born.
And as I crawled, my body
Resting warm against the ground,
I carefully breathed the autumn air
And skillfully made no sound

That would reveal my presence
To the neighbor, Mrs. Day
Who hummed a tune quite loudly
While behind her house I lay.
And then saw I the path that wound
Until it reached the sand.
And as I ran anticipation
Took me by the hand.
I smelled the ocean's breeze
As waves, like drums, did loudly beat
Against the cool, white sand
That felt so fine beneath my feet.
And there he stood majestically,
His mane dampened by the sea,
A golden horse whose gracefulness
My eyes rejoiced to see.
For it is rare that one so young
Can leave one's home and place,
To see the beach and mount a
Horse who only knows your face.
And since that day I haven't been
To walk along the beach,
For parents can become quite strict
When discipline they teach.
Yet I remember clearly how the
Horse did gently neigh
As I took leave and said
Farewell that bright September day!

CHANCES

She had a chance and lost it
Like winter loses fall.
Then once again the sun
Shone brightly through
The trees so tall,
For another chance,
So precious, nestled at her feet
And with fingers most unworthy
And a heart of strong deceit
She once more reached
To catch the chance,
But it flew quickly by
Towards more deserving catchers...
She gave a little sigh.

Carry Me

Carry me not
To the fire-filled place
Where everywhere is
A sinful face,
But to the land
Of love and joy
Oh, carry me there.

Spare my eyes
The awful sight
Of souls forever
In the night,
Who hang like bats
In darkest caves
Oh, spare my eyes.

Contain me not
With false replies
Speak quickly,
For the chanting dies
Oh, carry me
To any place
Just let me see
Another's face.

The Agnostic

Is there really the spirit,
Satan, who causes men to sin?
Is the battle with the Devil
The only one we must win?
Or is it man himself
Who causes evil on the earth?
Is this a human quality
Existing from man's birth?
And if there is no Satan,
And that is understood,
Then is there really the spirit
For all things that are good?

THE TWO BLACK MEN

The two men stood
Upon the hill,
The lucid sky was
Calm and still.
One man was black,
The other white.
The sun released
Its vibrant light.
The black man sat
Beside a brook
And read aloud
The Holy book.
The white man knew not
How to read
His life had been
Of crime and greed.
And he had killed
A man that day.
The black man kneeled
And began to pray.
The praying man was
Black of flesh

And thus he was not free.
The criminal was black of soul
Which people could not see.
The clouds began to fill with rain,
The sky began to gray.
The two black men walked
Down the hill to end another day.

Again, There Will Be

Again there will be sunshine
Though clouds are passing now.
And when a flower has wilted,
Again its seed will grow.
The night will once again depart,
Once more a bird will soar.
A peace perhaps will come
Or once again there will be war.

Anywhere

Outside
A light glows
It always shines near.
Inside
The darkness grows
And also the fear.
Somewhere
The light holds
The answers I seek.
Everywhere
The darkness spreads
And makes us weak.

Who Will Say?

Who will say that man is pure
Despite his life of sin?
Who will say he has a soul
And goodness lies therein?
Who will say the virgin child
Has not the evil seed?
Man will say these things each day,
A conscience he must feed.

The Lonely Shadow

All alone this shadow,
That darkens all the earth,
Hovering o'er the sunlight
That shines on every birth.
Shapeless, it shades always,
Yet has no living mate.
And no light ever hides it,
And it will never wait.

1987: THREE PROPHECIES
OF THE FUTURE

1.   The child with eyes of liquid brown
Sat on the velvet seat.
Her dress was blue with pockets
And dark sandals hugged her feet.
Her nose was small, her lips were red
Her hair was neatly curled.
She gazed out at the lively streets,
A free and peaceful world.

2.   Her small head ached with worry
As she walked into the house.
Her uniform was wrinkled, there were
Stains upon her blouse.
People always ordered her,
Her thoughts were not her own.
For Communists had stopped the
Freedom that her land had known.

3.   Her eyes were closed in peaceful rest
      She lay upon the ground.
      Everything was quiet, not an echo
      Nor a sound.
      She'll never see the sun or smell
      The sweetness of the air.
      Like everyone, she sleeps now
      There is no life anywhere.

Autumn and New York

We've spent each year together
And I'll miss you so.
The bitter sweetness of your face
All somber and golden, ready for snow.
The time has come but I can't get there too,
When the final movement of your music
Is heard flowing thru
All the streets and gutters,
As sooty leaves come down
Turning the park from orange
To yellow to brown.
Oh how I'll miss that moment,
When night again comes fast to cool the air
And New York and autumn
Have their reckless affair.

WALKS ON FIRE ISLAND

Days on Fire Island
The sea smelling breeze
Brushed my bare legs and arms
As I walked on the narrow boardwalk
That stretched beyond,
Sand hills and piney brush beneath.
I drew my wagon along.
The sea was on my right
Looking so calm,
So strong within.
The bay was on my left
Between the mainland and me.
I walked alone and barefoot
Not afraid of splinters
Feeling so alive.

BLACK BIRD

Black bird on the beach
Resting solitary on a nest of rocks.
I thought I was alone
And so did you.
You try to fly
Your wings slow down
You haven't risen.
You try to walk
Your velvet chest
Comes down before your legs.
You knew to come here,
You are dying.
You try again to walk.

Brave Beggar

A beggar on his knees
Has come clawing
At the shoes I wear.
He cannot see beyond
His need,
I cannot see
Beneath it.
Brave beggar pull me down.
Wash my face
With your anguish.
I want to know
How you live in me
And I in you.
Feed me the grapes
Of sorrows
That camouflage
The joy of your birth.

OUR FINALITY

Our finality ties us together.
Echoes from bones,
Long dry of blood,
Pierce newborn ears.
Thoughts that estranged
Our ancestors
Embalm withered brains.
We are buried apart,
But when tongues become ashes,
Our quiescence is indistinguishable.

March Poem

If you never look, you'll never see
And lost is lost
However masked it may be.
Networks of thoughts
That dress us so,
Then cloak and cover our bodies below.
And the search for identity
Surges ahead
While our needs from within
Must be fed.
What is right, what is wrong,
Or weak or strong?
Our brains are to think
While our hearts are to know,
And forgetting will cost us
Our natural flow.

Souls

In the quiet
Of the darkness
Souls tingle,
Beneath skin
Inside hearts
Stirring ceremoniously,
Surging as if
To crack the ribs
Which contain them.

Snobs

Snobs have nothing
Except being snobs.
The illusion of "above"
Hides the reality, alone.
People who can only mix with
"Certain" others, when the
Labels match,
Are empty inside,
Where no label fits.

REGRET

Only grief hurts more,
Only humans have it.
Once gone by that door,
Hindsight cannot soothe it.

THE BACKYARD

In the backyard
We explored our beginnings,
Digging to get to China.
You proposed when we were five
And I giggled awkwardly,
Pulling up tufts of grass.
I gave you more than half
Of my candy after you finished yours.
You let me put one of your teeth
Under my pillow
When I wanted that dime so bad.
You protected me from the yellow jackets
With a weeping willow branch,
And I put cool mud
On the sting you got.
Twenty-seven years ago,
I saw you last
So I don't know
The man you became
But the amber of our time together
Is buried somewhere in the backyard.

WHAT

What the hell is going on in Lebanon?
Burnt children in the streets,
Buried beneath the latest fashions.
People, old or not,
Digging for their memories.
What God could wish this
On His chosen?
Jesus? Allah? Adonai?
Which tenet justifies the bodies,
Or pieces of them,
That block the paths of those
Who carry the wounded?

HUMANKIND

Humankind...human cruel
You think you are so sharp,
So brilliant,
The pick of the litter of life.
Yet you can't even live
With dignity;
Only with weapons and fear.
The smartest animal of the lot
Hasn't figured out how to
Dismantle the arms...forever.
We alone can think of tomorrow,
And destroy it.

In Vain

We call you "science" now.
Another of your names,
But not the same.
We create it,
Log it in books,
Document findings.
It is under our control,
Unlike the matchless symmetry
Of snowflakes
Or roses.

Untitled

I want to say something poetic
That will make you feel something inside.
I want to prove that I'm brilliant
Just because I am someone with pride.
It is good, oh so good, to feel whole
With another instead of alone.
Life is more than I've ever imagined
And there's much more to me than I've known.

F Minor

Dusk falls within.
The fibers of my soul
Play in F minor,
A melody of
Tender notes.
While in this wood
Haunted by Thoreau
I think of you.
We dance now
To memory.

Playing Chopin

My fingers know you.
They purge the keyboard
Of your melancholy,
Striking notes that expose
Your fragile soul.
Haunting chords reveal
Our intimacy.

My Spirit

My spirit is seeping down
Into my bowels,
Beyond my awareness.
I try to fan its lingering ember.
Again, I must
Hoist it into flight.
We have a lifelong gestation.

Almost Spring

Branches against grey sky,
Speckled with promised buds.
A robin's prelude born
By winds on the brink of warmth.
Hope stirs from hibernating
In my soul
Love breaks the ground of my heart.

THE BACK DOCK

Solitary jetty, anchored
Beneath indigo waves,
Extending purposefully
Amidst moss covered rocks
Where ospreys retire.
I sit on one of two
Built-in benches
As the sun casts a
Final glow on this
Outpost for timeless dreams.
I sit here, long after I leave.

Words

Forty years brings no answers,
And fewer questions.
The little girl inside has
Always "known".
The woman understands.
"Why" is meaningless.
"That" is.
Words are like prehistoric,
Blunt edged weapons.
They slightly civilize.
The time will come
When they won't distract,
When they will mean.

The Sixties

We shall overcome.
We are flowing in every direction.
We're not like you anymore.
You're stiffer than corpses
And dimensionless.
That's why we snapped.
We couldn't learn from you
And we nearly perished
From your drought.
Instead we erupted,
Our hair like lava pouring forth.
Don't try to understand us
Or stop what we've become.
Take your place in the background.
There's room even for you.

THE SEVENTIES

Decade with no soul,
Birthed by the sixties but not of them.
Women grazed the range like men.
Men grew sideburns that covered nothing.
Even a President resigned.
Unhallowed time,
When a President was pardoned,
And Jim Jones served Kool-Aid
To thirsty men, women and children.

CAPITOL ISLAND

Tiny ladyfinger birthed by the sea.
Haven to feathered families
Landing on rock ledged borders
To dry their wings
And eat wriggling prey.
Children's children's children's
Summer play land.
Tree blessed refuge for the soul.

ONE SQUARE

I'm standing here,
Where I've always been
Even when I was gone.
I'm resting here,
Where it's always safe,
Even when pins fly.
I'm being here,
Where I've always known
I could live.

This Stillness

An untangled, soulful moment
Within,
This peace so infrequent,
So perfect
Like an airborne bubble.

WATCHING ICE MELT

Ice cubes in the kitchen sink
Crowding each other as they are
Dumped from the bucket
Making a clank sound
Like they do when
Dropped into a tall glass
Then suddenly hot water
From the faucet rains over them
And they start to melt
Dissolving into each other
Becoming each other
Until there is no other
Their fluid ghost
Swirling towards the drain
Traveling down a pipe and
On to the next state of being

THE PROMISE OF THE SUNRISE

With each sunrise there is hope.
The day begins unlived and possible.
The terror of the night beaten back
By the luminous, unstoppable sun.

Central Park

Tree womb
Bird womb
Soul womb
Home to benches
Named for those
Who loved you

The Life of a Bench

First it is built somewhere by someone,
Then painted dark green because
It will live in Central Park.
It is placed alongside other
Benches that border a
Footpath near the back of the Met.
The late morning sun will warm it.
Passers by, some tired some not,
Will sit for a long time or a moment.
One day a metal plaque engraved
With a loving message
Will be nailed on the bench's back,
The dedication of this one bench
To someone loved, honored,
Remembered, missed.

Two Flies

Two flies on a park bench, on the middle slat
Of the back part.
Two flies mating luxuriously, safely in the quiet
Afternoon light.
I am watching them with awe. I am
Protecting them with my presence,
No one will try to sit on this bench with me
Their intimacy is secure.
All these words, intimacy, secure,
Safe, bench, mating
Mean not one thing to them
Not to fly mounted upon fly, the latter's
Teeny legs wriggling on and off
The former seeming to have a hold
On the head of its' mount.
I presume the fly on top is the male, and I
Think maybe he is forcing himself upon
His mate. Is "her" wriggling pleasure or a
Desperate attempt to free herself?
The flies face forward and are attached at
Their rears, or so it seems to me.
Nature programs on television show
This kind of thing.

I wonder if the people filming those shows
Feel at all like I do now. Like a protector,
Like a voyeur?
Like I'm peeking, when I should turn away,
Let them have their privacy?
Even though that means not one thing to them.
What about what privacy means to me?
Would I want to be observed
Being mounted and penetrated, whether
Wanting it or submitting to it?

THE HARNESS

It's called a harness because it holds you back.
Sometimes you know you're in one,
Sometimes you just behave like you are.
Sometimes you keep acting
Like the harness is on
Long after it is gone.
If you're that used to being in the lane,
You won't cross the line
Even though it's only white paint on the road,
Easily stepped on, and over.

The Purge

I'm purging myself of fear,
A toxin I have lived with too long.
I'm purging it from
My stomach, jaw, brain,
Dreams, thoughts.
I flush the waste of fear
Into a sewer of my tears.

WITHOUT FEAR

I'm living my life without fear.
That's right, I'm finally here.
It took long enough
Sometimes it was rough
I had to keep checking
To make sure I was safe
But never could feel
That way
Until today.

MERMAID POWER

It fits in one hand
My mermaid
Made of leather and sequins
She says yes yes yes
In my hand
My hand becomes
Way more than that
It becomes a wand
Waving me forward
Here and now
Sweeping the clutter
Of what was
Away

Personal Peace

Elixir of being
The meaning in the search
Pot of gold
For the rainbow within
Not easy to experience
But worth the
Self weathered journey

Mountain Pose

Legs proud rooted
Chest the summit
Breath as strong
As a gale
Eyes wet with
Tears made from joy

Made in the USA
Middletown, DE
01 October 2015